MADAM
C. J. WALKER

The African-American Biographies Series

MAYA ANGELOU
More Than a Poet
0-89490-684-4

LOUIS ARMSTRONG
King of Jazz
0-89490-997-5

ARTHUR ASHE
Breaking the Color Barrier
in Tennis
0-89490-689-5

BENJAMIN BANNEKER
Astronomer and Mathematician
0-7660-1208-5

RALPH BUNCHE
Winner of the Nobel Peace Prize
0-7660-1203-4

W. E. B. DU BOIS
Champion of Civil Rights
0-7660-1209-3

DUKE ELLINGTON
Giant of Jazz
0-89490-691-7

ARETHA FRANKLIN
Motown Superstar
0-89490-686-0

WHOOPI GOLDBERG
Comedian and Movie Star
0-7660-1205-0

LORRAINE HANSBERRY
Playwright and Voice of Justice
0-89490-945-2

LANGSTON HUGHES
Poet of the
Harlem Renaissance
0-89490-815-4

ZORA NEALE HURSTON
Southern Storyteller
0-89490-685-2

QUINCY JONES
Musician, Composer, Producer
0-89490-814-6

BARBARA JORDAN
Congresswoman, Lawyer,
Educator
0-89490-692-5

CORETTA SCOTT KING
Striving for
Civil Rights
0-89490-811-1

MARTIN LUTHER KING, JR.
Leader for Civil Rights
0-89490-687-9

TONI MORRISON
Nobel Prize-Winning
Author
0-89490-688-7

WALTER DEAN MYERS
Writer for Real Teens
0-7660-1206-9

JESSE OWENS
Track and Field Legend
0-89490-812-X

COLIN POWELL
Soldier and Patriot
0-89490-810-3

PAUL ROBESON
Actor, Singer,
Political Activist
0-89490-944-4

JACKIE ROBINSON
Baseball's Civil Rights
Legend
0-89490-690-9

IDA B. WELLS-BARNETT
Crusader Against Lynching
0-89490-947-9

OPRAH WINFREY
Talk Show Legend
0-7660-1207-7

CARTER G. WOODSON
Father of African-American History
0-89490-946-0

—African-American Biographies—

MADAM
C. J. WALKER

Self-Made Businesswoman

Series Consultant:
Dr. Russell L. Adams, Chairman
Department of Afro-American Studies, Howard University

Della A. Yannuzzi

Enslow Publishers, Inc.

40 Industrial Road	PO Box 38
Box 398	Aldershot
Berkeley Heights, NJ 07922	Hants GU12 6BP
USA	UK

http://www.enslow.com

Dedicated to my friends
Kate, Cathey, Helen, Jani, Kathleen, and Terry

Copyright © 2000 by Della A. Yannuzzi

All rights reserved.

Library of Congress Cataloging-in-Publication Data

Yannuzzi, Della A.
    Madam C.J. Walker : self-made businesswoman / Della Yannuzzi.
        p.   cm. — (African-American biographies)
    Includes bibliographical references and index.
    Summary: A biography of the African-American woman who went from being a laundress to a self-made millionaire.
        ISBN 0-7660-1204-2
    1. Walker, C. J., Madam, 1867–1919   Juvenile literature.   2. Afro-American women   executives   Biography   Juvenile literature.   3. Cosmetics industry— United States—History   Juvenile literature.   [1. Walker, C. J., Madam, 1867–1919.   2. Businesswomen.   3. Afro-Americans Biography.   4. Women Biography.   5. Cosmetics industry—History.]   I. Title.   II. Series.
    HD9970.5.C672Y36   2000
    338.7'66855'092—dc21
    [B]   99-16447
                                                                    CIP
Printed in the United States of America

10 9 8 7 6 5 4 3 2 1

To Our Readers: All Internet addresses in this book were active and appropriate when we went to press. Any comments or suggestions can be sent by e-mail to Comments@enslow.com or to the address on the back cover.

Every effort has been made to locate all copyright holders of material used in this book. If any errors or omissions have occurred, corrections will be made in future editions of this book.

Illustration Credits: A'Lelia Bundles/Walker Family Collection, pp. 6, 61, 89; Courtesy of the Photographs and Prints Division, Schomberg Center for Research in Black Culture, The New York Public Library, Astor, Lenox and Tilden Foundations, p. 57; Ed Swiatkowski, p. 98; Library of Congress, pp. 17, 21, 32, 36, 41; Madam C. J. Walker Collection, Courtesy of the Indiana Historical Society, pp. 14, 28, 39, 43, 46, 53, 73, 77, 79, 80, 92; Special Collections and Archives, W.E.B. Du Bois Library, University of Massachusetts Amherst, p. 66.

Cover Illustration: A'Lelia Bundles/Walker Family Collection

Contents

Sarah Breedlove McWilliams: "Madam C. J. Walker"

1

SARAH'S VISION

When Sarah Breedlove McWilliams, at the age of thirty-seven, went to the 1904 World's Fair in St. Louis, Missouri, she attended a meeting of the National Association of Colored Women (NACW). There, McWilliams listened with great interest to a speech given by Margaret Murray Washington. Margaret Washington was the wife of the well-known African-American educator Booker T. Washington.

Margaret Washington was a hardworking member of the NACW. The goals of this powerful organization were to offer financial help, medical assistance, opportunities for education, and whatever else was needed to assist African-American women and their families. The motto of the NACW was "Lifting as We Climb." The group had been created in 1885 with the merging of the National Federation of Afro-American Women, made up of thirty-six African-American women's clubs in twelve states, and another organization, the National Colored Woman's League.

As McWilliams watched and listened to this stylish, attractive woman, she was impressed with Washington's self-confidence and speaking skills. Most of all, she noticed that Washington's personal appearance was outstanding. Her clothes were fashionable and fit well, and her thick hair was glowing with health. Although McWilliams always wore clean skirts and starched white blouses, her hair, unlike Washington's, was thinning and without shine. Years of a poor diet and the use of a wrap-and-twist method to straighten her curly hair had damaged it. She and many other African-American women were experiencing the same unsightly problems—bald patches, dandruff, and diseases of the scalp.

After listening to Washington's speech, McWilliams left the NACW meeting with renewed energy and determination to improve her own life. For more than twenty years, she had earned a meager $1.50 a week by washing and ironing other people's clothes. She had managed to save enough money to send her only child,

A'Lelia, to a private African-American college in Knoxville, Tennessee. But now it was time to think about her own future. She was getting older and more tired each day from bending over big tubs of soapy, hot water.

Besides washing clothes, McWilliams had a job selling hair care products door-to-door for a St. Louis business called the Poro Company. She had used some of the Poro products on her own damaged hair but did not see much improvement. She started to wonder whether she could develop her own line of hair care products and begin her own hair care business. She decided to learn all she could about the beauty business.[1]

McWilliams gained valuable work experience in her job for Poro. She learned about sales promotion, door-to-door selling, and the beauty and hair care industry. McWilliams also began to pray for help and support. She wanted some guidance to make her dream come true. Then, one day in early 1905, she announced to some friends that her prayers had been answered. She said, "One night I had a dream, and in that dream a big black man appeared to me and told me what to mix up for my hair. . . . I mixed it, and put it on my scalp, and in a few weeks my hair was coming in faster than it had ever fallen out. I made up my mind I would begin to sell it."[2]

McWilliams's dream had told her that some of the things she needed to put in her hair mixture were grown in Africa. She believed so much in her vision that she sent away for the ingredients. Over the next few weeks, McWilliams began to experiment with different hair mixtures. She tried them on her own hair and that of her friends. Her secret hair mixture worked so well that she decided to sell it. She also created a variation on a steel comb used by French beauticians. When heated and used with one of her hair products, the comb straightened curly hair.

In July 1905, McWilliams decided to leave St. Louis, where the Poro Company had a large share of the hair care business. She moved to Denver, Colorado. Her plan was to sell her hair care products in Denver, where there would be less competition from other African-American hair care companies.

In Denver, she would also be near her widowed sister-in-law, who had four daughters. McWilliams wanted a fresh start and a new place to begin her business. She said good-bye to her friends, including Charles Joseph Walker, a sales agent for a local newspaper. Her belongings consisted of one suitcase and $1.50 in savings.

McWilliams had high hopes for her new life in Colorado. Although the African-American population in Denver was smaller than that in St. Louis, she pushed ahead with her plans to build a business in the beautiful mile-high city. First, she found a job as a cook for a drugstore owner named E. L. Scholtz. In her free time—likely with some help from her employer, who was familiar with chemicals—she developed three hair care products. She called them Wonderful Hair Grower, Glossine, and Vegetable Shampoo. The first product, Wonderful Hair Grower, had the same name as one of the Poro Company products. McWilliams began to sell her products door-to-door, dressed in a crisp white shirt and a long, dark skirt.[3]

Six months after moving to Denver, Walker married Charles Joseph Walker. They had kept in touch by writing letters. McWilliams, now Mrs. Charles Joseph (C. J.) Walker, decided to use the name Madam C. J. Walker because it had a dignified sound to it. Within six years, the Madam C. J. Walker Manufacturing Company would be earning more than $100,000 a year, a huge sum of money in the early 1900s.

Walker liked to say, "I got myself a start by giving myself a start."[4] This philosophy helped to put the hardworking single mother on the road to becoming America's first female African-American millionaire. Her belief that African-American women could succeed in business set an example for many women who followed in her footsteps. If Sarah Breedlove McWilliams could work her way up from washtubs to the presidency of her own company, then maybe others could also achieve success.

2

THE ALMOST-
CHRISTMAS BABY

arah Breedlove was born in Delta, Louisiana, on December 23, 1867, on a cotton plantation owned by Robert W. Burney. The plantation was named Grand View because of its view of Vicksburg, a city on the other side of the Mississippi River. Sarah was born a free child, but her parents had been slaves. Owen and Minerva Breedlove were two of the 4 million enslaved African Americans freed at the end of the Civil War.[1]

Minerva Breedlove had worked in the cotton fields up until the day of Sarah's birth. Sarah's family also included an older brother, Alex, and a sister, Louvenia.

The Breedloves were so poor that they could not afford any Christmas gifts that year.

Sarah was not quite seven months old when the Fourteenth Amendment to the Constitution was passed into law by Congress. The amendment stated that all African Americans were citizens of the United States and were entitled to the rights and equal protection guaranteed by the Constitution. However, this law did not always work.

After the bitter Civil War, the South had to be rebuilt. This transition period was called Reconstruction. Slowly, African Americans would move out of slavery and into the free world, but this would take time and the efforts of many people.

The Breedloves could have left the Burney plantation, but they decided to stay on after the war. They were simply too poor to go anywhere else. They worked as sharecroppers, renting land from Robert Burney and farming it by planting and picking cotton. Typically, sharecroppers had to give one half to two thirds of their crops to the landowner and then could sell whatever was left to bring in a little cash. It was a difficult way to make a living, especially when cotton prices dropped, there was a bad crop, or a landowner was dishonest.

Life on the Burney plantation was hard for the Breedloves. Their home was a one-room cabin with only wooden shutters over the window openings to keep out the winter winds. The family slept on the dirt floor. The only heat to warm the cabin came from the fireplace, where the Breedloves also cooked their meals.

From 1865 to 1877—the Reconstruction period—the federal government was attempting to help rebuild the local economies. The government also sought to improve social relations between the races and to include African Americans in society. Congress created the Freedmen's Bureau to help in the transition. Health, legal, and educational services were made

Walker was born in this one-room cabin on a cotton plantation in Delta, Louisiana.

available to people who had been slaves. Many former slaves became tenant farmers, and some others went into business with government aid. Unfortunately, the Breedlove family did not benefit from the government's efforts to better people's lives. It was difficult to break away from the chains of prejudice and poverty.

Everyone in the Breedlove family worked in the cotton fields. From the age of five, Sarah was put to work: first in her house and then later in the fields. She gathered eggs from the chickens, collected firewood, weeded the garden, and helped prepare the breakfast and dinner meals. The hardest work, though, was in the cotton fields. Cotton cultivation began in March with seeding, hoeing, and weeding. It lasted through August, when the last cotton was picked. Then the cotton fibers were separated from the seeds and baled.

Sarah spent long hours in the hot sun picking many pounds of cotton. Pickers had large sacks slung over their shoulders as they walked through the fields gathering the valuable crop. There were many times when Sarah came home with dozens of cuts on her fingers from plucking the cotton blossoms out of their prickly hard brown pods. There were no child labor laws at that time to protect children from working all day long at difficult jobs.

Sarah's parents wanted their children to go to school, but they were needed at home and in the cotton fields. The whole family struggled and sacrificed to put food on the table and keep a roof over their heads. As Sarah grew older, she was given more demanding chores. Her family earned extra money by taking in other people's laundry. Minerva Breedlove taught her daughters, Sarah and Louvenia, how to wash clothes. On weekends the three of them would scrub and beat the dirt out of bedsheets, tablecloths, heavy overalls, and shirts. Clothes had to be soaked and stirred in large wooden tubs filled with hot water and harsh soap made from lye, a caustic chemical. It was a grueling task for a grown woman, and even more so for young girls like Sarah and her sister. For washing clothes, the family earned about $1 a week.

When Sarah was seven years old, a terrible tragedy occurred that changed her life forever: Her mother and father died. Although the cause of their death is not known for certain, some reports have said that they may have died during an epidemic of yellow fever, a deadly disease spread by mosquitoes.[2]

The Breedlove children were left orphans with only one another for comfort. They missed the love, warmth, and security that they had received from their parents. Still, although they were poor, at least they had a home. They had no choice except to stay on the Burney plantation and try to work the land. Sarah and Louvenia also continued to wash other people's clothes to bring in more money. Eventually, Sarah's

Picking cotton all day long in the hot sun was a difficult way to earn a living.

brother, Alex, left his sisters to move to Vicksburg, Mississippi, the busy city across the river. He wanted to find a job with better pay.

Sarah and Louvenia stayed behind on the plantation. Throughout the week, they tended the cotton fields, earning only about fifty cents a day. On weekends, they washed clothes. Sarah dreamed of going to school and maybe traveling around the country.[3] Instead, she only worked harder. Four years later, in 1878, Sarah and Louvenia had to give up their one-room cabin. Their cotton crop had failed, and the girls could no longer afford the rent. They followed Alex's example and moved to Vicksburg. The city was overcrowded and plagued with an epidemic of yellow fever. Louvenia found a job washing clothes, and Sarah soon joined her in doing the same work.

Sarah and Louvenia were lucky to find employment in Vicksburg. Many African Americans were crowding into the city to find any kind of job. Their opportunities were limited. In the late 1800s, African-American women were limited to being washerwomen, cooks, nurses, seamstresses, and servants.

Not long after moving to Vicksburg, Louvenia married a man named Willie Powell. Sarah lived with her sister and brother-in-law in a chilly, dark shack. Sarah did not like her sister's husband. He had a bad temper and was cruel to both Sarah and Louvenia. Sarah endured this hard life for three years because there was nothing else she could do. Then, in 1882, at the age of fourteen, Sarah met a kind man named Moses (Jeff) McWilliams. She married him and moved out of her sister's house. Sarah was finally going to have a home of her own.[4]

3

A HOME OF
HER OWN

Sarah Breedlove McWilliams knew that her new husband did not have any money, but Moses McWilliams had offered her the chance to have a home.[1] He was a hardworking man who took whatever jobs he could find in the crowded city. Sarah spent long hours bending over a water-filled wooden tub, scrubbing and washing other people's clothes. It was work she knew well because she had been doing it since she was seven years old.

Sarah and her husband struggled to make ends meet. After two years, Sarah had her first and only child, Lelia McWilliams, born on June 6, 1885.[2] Lelia became the center of Sarah's world. Sarah wanted nothing more than to give her daughter a better life.

Sarah and Moses tried to save some of their hard-earned money for Lelia's future. Then, one day, another tragedy occurred in Sarah's life: Moses was killed, perhaps in an accident, though the details of his death are not known.[3] What is known is that at the age of nineteen, Sarah Breedlove McWilliams was a widow and a single mother. What would she do?

McWilliams could not take time to mourn her husband. She was now the sole support for herself and Lelia. Finding work in Vicksburg was becoming more difficult. New people kept moving into the city, and they were willing to take whatever jobs were available, even at very low wages. McWilliams heard from her neighbors that she could probably find better-paying work in St. Louis, Missouri.[4]

In 1888, McWilliams and Lelia traveled by riverboat to St. Louis, a city of half a million people, and made their way to the African-American community. The two of them became a part of the city's black population of about thirty-five thousand. There were three black newspapers and more than one hundred black-owned businesses in St. Louis. McWilliams found a room for herself and Lelia in a boardinghouse. Then she started to look for work. Since she had experience as a laundrywoman, she did not have any trouble finding a job. She did not want to wash clothes for a living, but it was something she could do at home. She had to be there to take care of Lelia, who was still too young to attend school.

McWilliams washed, starched, and ironed clothes seven days a week, up to fourteen hours a day. When she was finished with the baskets of clothes, she had to deliver them to her customers. That meant walking through the city streets carrying the finished laundry.

Although there was not much time for a social life, McWilliams did join St. Paul African Methodist Episcopal Church. The members of the church

Like the woman in this photograph, Walker worked seven days a week, often fourteen hours a day, washing other people's clothes.

welcomed her. She returned their kindness by joining the St. Paul's Mite Missionary Society, whose members volunteered to help needy people in the St. Louis community.

McWilliams also attended night school, where she began to learn how to read and write. During this time she married again. Her new husband, John Davis, was a heavy drinker, and the marriage did not last long. McWilliams divorced him during Lelia's high school years.[5]

After she finished high school, Lelia attended Knoxville College in Tennessee. McWilliams had always planned to send her only child to college. She had saved every penny she could since the day Lelia was born. Now, with that goal met, McWilliams turned her attention to improving her own life.

McWilliams was in her midthirties and still washing and ironing for a living. She had always tried to take care of her appearance, but her hands were chapped and rough from soaking in hot soapy water for nearly thirty years. Her scalp was dry, and her hair was thinning. One day, as she was bent over the washboard with her arms deep in soapsuds, she said to herself, "What are you going to do when you grow old and your back gets stiff? This set me to thinking, but with all my thinking, I couldn't see how I, a poor washerwoman, was going to better my condition."[6]

In 1904, McWilliams gained some inspiration when

she visited the World's Fair in St. Louis and listened to Margaret Murray Washington speak to the St. Louis branch of the National Association of Colored Women, (NACW). McWilliams was in awe of the stylish and well-groomed wife of Booker T. Washington. McWilliams admired Washington's confidence and speaking skills, but most of all she was impressed with Washington's appearance. Her hair, especially, was thick and vibrant-looking. McWilliams left the NACW meeting more determined than ever to do something besides laundry for other people.

McWilliams was not the first African-American woman who had problems with the health and management of her hair. Nor was she the first to recognize that hair products made especially for the needs of African-Americans could help solve those problems. In the early 1900s, an African-American woman named Annie Turnbo Malone had begun her own hair care company. Her company manufactured the products and then marketed them door-to-door. Malone named her business the Poro Company. The West African word *poro* means a group or organization devoted to physical and spiritual well-being. In addition to washing clothes, McWilliams sold hair care products door-to-door for the Poro Company.

McWilliams and Annie Turnbo Malone had common life experiences and goals. Both were born after slavery was abolished. Malone, born in 1869, was two years younger than McWilliams. She was the tenth of eleven children and was raised on a farm in Metropolis, Illinois. Her family was poor, and like McWilliams, Malone had been orphaned at a young age. A sister raised her in Peoria, Illinois, sending her to both grade school and high school. McWilliams, on the other hand, did not attend school as a child. Later, though, she made up for her lack of education by enrolling in night school and by hiring private tutors. Both McWilliams and Malone were determined to succeed. They recognized that African-American women cared about their appearance, and they created hair products especially formulated for African-American women.

McWilliams had been living in St. Louis for four years before Annie T. Malone moved there and started her own company. While the Poro Company was advertising its products, hiring sales agents, and increasing sales throughout the Midwest, McWilliams was still earning a living washing and ironing clothes. Malone already had an established business when McWilliams decided to start her own hair care company, but McWilliams would quickly catch up with her competition. She combined her own desire to succeed with the experience she gained working for the Poro Company. This turned out to be a winning combination.

4

SARAH'S INVENTION

arah McWilliams knew that other African-American women were also suffering from thinning hair and patches of alopecia, or baldness. Poor diet and nutrition, a lack of time to take care of their hair, and overuse of hair-straightening techniques contributed to their hair problems. Many African-American women ironed their hair with a hot iron to straighten it. This often damaged or burned their hair and caused it to fall out. Another popular straightening technique was the wrap-and-twist method. This consisted of dividing hair into sections, wrapping string tightly around each section, and then twisting the section. The hair was less curly when combed out, but overuse of this method caused scalp problems and hair loss. McWilliams began working on hair remedies to treat the scalp and achieve healthy, shiny hair.

McWilliams decided to establish her business in Denver, Colorado, where there would be less competition from similar products. In July 1905, she arrived alone in the growing city, where her widowed sister-in-law and four nieces lived. McWilliams's daughter, Lelia, was in college and would join her after graduation. Although McWilliams had very little money in her purse—just $1.50, a week's wages for washing clothes—she was ready and eager to pursue her dream. She was confident that her hair care products would fill a need in Denver's small African-American community.

McWilliams rented a room in a boardinghouse, and established herself in the church community. She joined the Shorter Chapel African Methodist Episcopal Church, where she became active in helping the area's poor people. She also found work as a cook in the home of E. L. Scholtz, a pharmacist and owner of a large drugstore. Her employer helped her learn more about medicines and different remedies that could be useful in improving African-American women's hair.[1] In her spare time, she worked on her hair formulas.

The secret ingredient in McWilliams's hair formula

was probably sulfur, which was known to have healing properties. When combined with other ingredients, it would moisturize and soften hair and cure dandruff. McWilliams experimented with the mixture, continually testing it on her own hair, as well as on the heads of her nieces and willing friends. When McWilliams's hair loss stopped, and the texture and brightness of her hair improved, she decided she was ready to sell the hair care formula to other women.[2]

McWilliams had perfected three hair care products. She packaged them in glass jars and began selling them door-to-door. Later, her products would be sold in tin containers with her name and face stamped on the front.

The first product she developed was called Wonderful Hair Grower. Like Annie Turnbo Malone's product with the same name, it was designed to stop hair loss and to encourage new hair growth. The second product, Glossine, was a light oil that straightened the hair and gave lackluster hair a beautiful shine. The third product was Vegetable Shampoo, used to cleanse the scalp and hair and to remove dandruff. McWilliams had also designed a steel comb based on an existing French one. Her comb had wide gaps between the teeth and was meant for use on thick, curly hair. This comb was to be heated over a stove or open flame and used with the Glossine to press and straighten hair.[3]

One of Walker's first products was Wonderful Hair Grower. The box featured a picture of Walker herself—with lush, thick hair after using this product.

Although Sarah McWilliams was a busy woman, she found the time to marry for a third time. On January 4, 1906, six months after moving to Denver, she married Charles Joseph (C. J.) Walker, her friend from St. Louis. McWilliams, now Mrs. C. J. Walker, began calling herself Madam C. J. Walker. She decided to use it as her company name because she believed that it looked and sounded like a respectable, important name.

Charles Walker had been a sales agent for a St. Louis newspaper and was experienced in the world of advertisement and promotion. While his wife was selling her products door-to-door and offering free demonstrations by washing customers' hair and then applying her products, he was handling the promotion side of her new business and helping to expand the mail-order sales. Walker advertised and sold his wife's products through the mail, advertising in the *Colorado Statesman* newspaper, in flyers, and through posters.

Drugstores, retail shops, and department stores were not included as markets for her products, however, because the shopkeepers did not want to carry products made specifically for black people. Charles Walker also helped his wife create a medicinal product, C. J. Walker's Blood and Rheumatic Remedy.

When Lelia graduated from college, she joined her mother in Denver and helped with the business. Walker encouraged Lelia and the other women in the Walker family to become involved in her company. As long as they expressed an interest in the business, Madam Walker was ready to give them jobs. Lelia, her cousins, and aunt processed orders. Walker's sister, Louvenia, worked in the product-packaging division. Walker was proud of all of them, but she was especially pleased with her only child. Lelia had grown into a tall, stunning woman with a strong talent for business. The Madam C. J. Walker Manufacturing Company continued to prosper under the direction of Madam Walker and the other Walker women.

To make her company grow, Madam Walker was willing to take big risks. In September 1906, she hired a touring car and took a sales trip around the country to promote her hair care products. She was on the road for a year and a half. Traveling around the United States to market her products was "a pioneering act," says Betty Collier Thomas, a historian at Temple University.[4] Walker's husband, Charles, and others did not expect the sales trip to succeed at all. They were very wrong.

Walker set out to visit New York, Oklahoma, Louisiana, and six other states. Her goal was to increase her business from $10 a week to perhaps $20 or $25 a week. She surprised even herself by bringing in $35 a week after just a few months. (White men at that time earned less than half that amount.) During this trip, she was also sending sales orders back home to Denver to be filled by her daughter, Lelia, and nieces, Anjetta, Thirsapen, Mattie, and Gladis. Even with all the helping hands, Lelia and the other family members were finding it difficult to keep up with the incoming business.

By 1908, Walker's company had opened the doors

of opportunity for other African-American women to enter the competitive world of business. In addition to selling and promoting her products, Madam Walker was also recruiting saleswomen to sell her Walker Hair Care System to other women. In return, Walker agents earned a share of the company's profits. She was proud to say, "I have made it possible for many colored women to abandon the washtub for a more pleasant and profitable occupation."[5]

Walker's business was flourishing, but it was not without criticism. Many African Americans thought Walker was promoting a white woman's look, which was a style of long, straight hair. Some black ministers attacked her from the pulpit. "If God meant for blacks to have straight hair, he would have endowed them with it," they said.[6]

Walker had always felt a strong sense of racial pride and responded to these criticisms by saying, "Let me correct the erroneous impression held by some that I claim to straighten hair. I deplore such an impression because I have always held myself out as a hair culturist. I grow hair."[7]

Walker passionately believed that for black women to gain respect and succeed in a white-run world, a good appearance was crucial. She not only sold products, she also promoted her philosophy: "I want the great masses of people to take greater pride in their

Walker's hair care formulas made her own hair soft and shiny and glowing with health.

personal appearance and to give their hair proper attention."[8]

By the spring of 1908, when Walker was forty-one years old, her company was earning close to $400 per month. This was a large amount of money at that time. The business was growing so quickly that she began to look for a new location for the company.

5

A FAMILY
BUSINESS

In 1908, Madam Walker decided to make the bustling city of Pittsburgh, Pennsylvania, her new headquarters. Walker quickly established herself in the African-American business community there. She rented office space in a building on Wylie Avenue, the main street of the African-American community. Walker and her daughter, who came to Pittsburgh that summer, worked together on their plans to expand the Madam C. J. Walker Manufacturing Company.

The two Walker women opened a beauty salon and then founded a training school for Walker beauty culturists. Madam Walker named the school Lelia College after her daughter. The school quickly filled with applicants from all walks of life who were eager to be trained in the Walker Hair Care System. Instruction at Lelia College included reading materials, such as training booklets, and hands-on training. The beauty agents learned how to properly apply the Walker products in training sessions. They also learned the techniques used in selling door-to-door. Walker told her agents how to dress when they were selling her products. They had to wear a black skirt and a white starched blouse and must always be neat and well groomed.

Walker and her daughter trained hundreds of women at the college as well as through a $25 hair care correspondence course. Graduates of Lelia College were given certificates of achievement stating that they were qualified Walker Hair Culturists.

An important lesson in the teaching of the Walker Hair Care System was how to achieve and maintain good hygiene and healthy hair care. Many African-American women wanted manageable, straightened hair. However, if they had scalp diseases or their hair was falling out, then straightening the hair alone would not solve their hair problems. Walker encouraged her students to teach future customers about the importance of a well-groomed appearance, which included a healthy, shiny head of hair. One of Walker's

Madam Walker also taught women to improve their looks with smartly manicured nails and clothes that were clean and neat.

most popular hair products was Vegetable Shampoo because it promoted a healthy scalp.

Lelia College opened the doors for many African-Americans to become independent businesswomen. Walker was proud of the fact that she was giving employment to thousands of women who now had an opportunity beyond working as washerwomen, cooks, and housekeepers.[1] Over the years, Walker also tried to offer work opportunities to African-American men. Later, when her employees needed housing, she hired African-American men to build homes for them. She explained her philosophy in this way: "My business is largely supported by my own people, so why shouldn't

I spend my money so that it will go back into colored homes?"[2]

In 1909, Lelia married John Robinson, a hotel worker in Pittsburgh. She continued to work with her mother. By 1910, Walker's company employed almost a thousand agents throughout the United States. The Walker agents earned a commission on their sales. This means they earned a certain amount of money for each product they sold.

Madam Walker was always looking for ways to expand her business and increase sales. She wanted her company to become even bigger and better. On one of her sales trips, she had stopped in Indianapolis, Indiana. The city had a good railroad system and offered many manufacturing and business opportunities. Walker had met an Indianapolis newsman—an African-American, George L. Knox—who suggested that she move to the city. After carefully thinking about the advantages of moving her business headquarters there, Walker decided to make the change. She left Lelia in charge of the Pittsburgh office and beauty school.

Part of Walker's business success resulted from her sharp ability to select the best people to work with her. Since she was always on the road, promoting her products, she needed someone to handle the daily operation of the new Indianapolis office. She chose Freeman B. Ransom, an African-American graduate of

Columbia University's law school, whom she had met a few years before. He was now living and working in Indianapolis. Ransom agreed to become Walker's general manager, attorney, and second-in-command.[3] She also hired Robert Lee Brokenburr, another lawyer, who became the assistant manager and legal advisor.

Walker knew she had to have capable and trustworthy employees to help run her company. On many of her sales trips, she met interesting and talented people. Sometimes she offered them jobs. One of those people was a Kentucky schoolteacher named Alice Kelly, who eventually was put in charge of Walker's Indiana factory. Kelly also became Walker's traveling companion and private tutor. She helped Walker improve her reading and writing skills. In September 1911, Walker legally incorporated her business. She remained principal owner and the company's sole stockholder.

The thriving Indianapolis business community welcomed Madam Walker and her hair care company. There were other established black businesses in this thriving city, but the Walker company managed to find its place among them. Walker's first home in Indianapolis consisted of living quarters, a small manufacturing plant, and a beauty salon. Walker and her management team settled in for a long and prosperous future.

Within a short time after moving to Indianapolis,

Walker decided she needed a larger building for her booming business. She came to this conclusion in an unexpected way after going to the Isis Theater one day to see a movie. When Walker placed her dime on the counter, the ticket clerk told her that movies now cost 25 cents for African Americans. Walker was so angry over this unfair treatment that she took immediate action: She made an appointment to see an architect.

Walker had planned to build a larger company

Walker poses on the steps of her new home on busy North West Street in Indianapolis, Indiana.

headquarters sometime in the future, but the movie theater incident prompted her to do it sooner. Her plans called for offices, beauty shops, a manufacturing plant, and a large movie theater for Indianapolis's African-American population. When it was completed a few years later, the new Madam C. J. Walker Manufacturing Company took up a full block in downtown Indianapolis.

Although Walker did not have much free time for hobbies or movies, she did enjoy music, art, and the theater. She also liked to drive her electric car around the city. This car could go up to thirty miles an hour and was able to travel for fifty miles on one battery charge. Now that Walker could afford some luxuries in life, she treated herself to a baby grand piano, a harp, and a phonograph. She also showed her support for African-American artists by buying their work. After so many years of being poor, Walker found pleasure in spending the money she was earning.

In addition to being generous to herself and to her family, she was even more giving to people outside her family. Walker wanted to contribute to the community and to those less fortunate than herself. She often donated money to homes for the aged and to African-American charities. She also enjoyed speaking to groups of people about her success. She once said at a National Negro Business League convention, "I am a woman who came from the cotton fields of the South.

I was promoted from there to the washtub. Then I was promoted to the cook kitchen, and from there I promoted myself into the business of manufacturing hair goods and preparations. . . . I have built my own factory on my own ground."[4]

Walker's business life was going well, but her marriage to C. J. Walker was in trouble. For a while, Walker and her husband had made a good team. In the beginning, Charles Walker was eager to help his wife with her company. Madam Walker had big plans for her business, but her husband soon realized he did not share his wife's desire to keep expanding the company.

"I have built my own factory on my own ground": Madam Walker's first factory in Indianapolis in 1911.

He was content with its current operation and did not want to take any big risks.

Madam Walker gave some serious thought to her personal and business life. She analyzed her marital situation this way: "I had business disagreements with him, for when we began to make ten dollars a day, he thought that amount was enough and that I should be satisfied. But I was convinced that my hair preparations would fill a long-felt want, and when we found it impossible to agree, due to his narrowness of vision, I embarked in business for myself."[5]

In 1912, Walker divorced her husband, but she kept his name. In their personal lives they went their separate ways, but Charles Walker continued to work for the business for the rest of his life, selling his former wife's hair care products.

At this time, Walker's daughter, A'Lelia (she had added the *A'* to her name) Walker Robinson, decided to add a new member to the family. She was now divorced from her husband and had no children. She wanted to adopt a thirteen-year-old girl named Mae Bryant. She had met the young girl when Mae was doing some errands for the Walker company. Mae was asked to do some modeling for the Walker products because she had long, beautiful thick hair.

Mae came from a poor family. She was a bright girl, and A'Lelia Robinson could offer her a promising future. Robinson asked Mae's widowed mother, Etta

Bryant, if she could adopt Mae. She promised her that Mae would get a college education, fine clothes, trips, and the personal attention of A'Lelia and Madam Walker. It was a difficult decision, but Etta Bryant finally agreed to let A'Lelia adopt her daughter. She wanted Mae to have a good life.

Madam Walker was thrilled to have a granddaughter. She took Mae with her on promotional trips around the country. Mae helped her adoptive grandmother by handing out flyers and by modeling

Madam Walker had big plans for her business. She soon expanded her line of beauty products to include face creams, powders, soaps, and toothpaste.

for Walker hair care products. In return, Mae had the best of everything, from expensive clothes, tutors, and vacations to a future filled with financial security for herself and her birth family. Mae was warmly welcomed into a loving and successful family. She would make a place for herself alongside the other Walker women.

6

GROWING BIGGER AND BETTER

Madam C. J. Walker was quickly achieving success. Because of her hard work, determination, and the self-promotion of her hair care system, the Walker company was continuing to grow bigger and better. By the end of 1912, Madam Walker's sixteen hundred agents were bringing in a total of $1,000 weekly. The numbers would continue to grow over the years. Walker herself traveled to hundreds of towns and cities around the country. Her daily schedule was filled with speaking engagements. Madam Walker was an energetic and persuasive speaker. At six feet tall, she was an impressive figure, beautifully dressed and perfectly groomed.[1] Walker's own appearance and healthy hair were the best advertisement for her products.

Walker spoke at churches and for women's groups, attended business conferences and conventions, and made appearances at public gatherings. She always had plenty of pamphlets and hair care samples to hand out to potential customers. Most important, Walker was generous with her time. She talked to anyone who wanted to learn more about her company and its financial opportunities.

On one of her trips, Walker met a respected African-American woman named Mary McLeod Bethune, a well-known educator. Walker and Bethune

Before and after: Walker's own appearance and healthy hair were offered as proof of her products' ability to improve dry and thinning hair.

crossed paths at a meeting of the National Association of Colored Women in Hampton, Virginia, in the summer of 1912. Walker was drawn to education, and a friendship with Bethune developed. Walker's secretary, Violet Reynolds, later said, "Madam Walker respected education because she lacked it. That's why she was so attracted to Mary McLeod Bethune. Bethune had the education, but Madam had the money, so they made a good team."[2]

Walker was so impressed with this hardworking woman's dedication to educating African-American children that she promised to raise money for Bethune's school in Daytona Beach, Florida.

Although Walker and Bethune were in different fields, they had many similarities in their lives. They were both born in poverty to former slaves. Bethune, born in 1875 in Maysville, South Carolina, was eight years younger than Walker. Bethune was more fortunate than Walker because she did not have to work in the cotton fields as a young child. She was allowed to go to school, walking five miles there and five miles home every day. When she was fifteen, her education stopped. She had to stay home to help earn money to pay the mortgage on her father's farm. Eventually, Bethune was offered an opportunity to go back to school. After graduation, she found a job as a teacher and was able to help her father pay off his debts.

Walker and Bethune rose out of poverty. They did

not let life's hardships stop them from following their dreams. Both women accomplished their goals by relying on their talents, inner strengths, and self-confidence. Walker moved to a new town with a dream of creating a successful business. Bethune rented a run-down cottage to use as a school. She raised the $11 a month she needed for rent by selling pies and ice cream to workmen. Her first school had just six students, and one of them was her son. She charged a weekly tuition of 50 cents.

Bethune later went on to buy some Daytona Beach property that had been a dumping area. She placed a $5 deposit on the land, which was priced at $250, and agreed to pay the rest in two years. Her first building was called Faith Hall. Bethune was only twenty-nine years old in 1904 when she started her school, which became known as the Daytona Normal and Industrial Institute for Negro Girls. In 1923, it merged with the Cookman Institute and became known as the Bethune-Cookman College. Bethune died in 1955, two months before her eightieth birthday, and was buried on the college grounds. Today, the school she started has more than two thousand students and nearly two hundred faculty members.

Although Bethune and many other black women congratulated Walker on her successful business career, Walker sometimes had to fight for recognition within the African-American business community. In 1912, she attended the convention of the National Negro Business League (NNBL). She was looking forward to hearing the stories of other successful African-American businesspeople. She also wanted the opportunity to speak to the members of the NNBL about her own success. Although most of the attendees were African-American men, she was certain that Booker T. Washington, the NNBL's president would permit her to speak at the convention. His wife, Margaret Murray Washington, was the woman whose speech had inspired Walker at the National Association of Colored Women meeting in 1904.

Booker Taliaferro Washington had been born a slave in 1856 in Franklin County, Virginia. His father was a white slaveowner, and his mother was a slave. He had an older brother, John, and a younger sister, Amanda. After President Abraham Lincoln's Emancipation Proclamation became effective on January 1, 1863, Booker and his family were freed from slavery. The Emancipation Proclamation freed slaves in states that had joined the Confederacy in the Civil War and had withdrawn from the Union. The Thirteenth Amendment to the Constitution finally freed all slaves throughout the United States.

Booker and his family moved to Malden, West Virginia, in 1865. Booker had a desire to learn, and he was able to attend school for a short time. Then his mother died, and he had to go to work in the salt and coal mines. He was only nine years old. In 1870, at the age of fourteen, Booker found work as a house servant for the mine owner's wife, Viola Ruffner. She believed in education and helped Booker to read and study.

In 1872, at the age of sixteen, Booker set off on a five-hundred-mile journey to Hampton Institute in Hampton, Virginia. He had only 50 cents in his pocket when he arrived, but he was determined to get an education. He paid his way through school by working as a janitor. In 1875, he graduated with honors from the institute and became a teacher.

In 1881, Washington was named principal of the school he founded, the new Normal School for black students in Tuskegee, Alabama. He taught thirty students in a shed donated by a black church. The shed was used until a school building could be built. In 1900, Washington went on to found the National Negro Business League. His school also continued to expand, and its name was changed to the Tuskegee Normal and Industrial Institute. By 1915, enrollment had grown to four thousand students studying a variety of practical job skills like carpentry and farming. The school became a world-famous center for agricultural research.

Washington believed that to improve their lives, people had to rely on themselves. He advised African Americans to "cast down your bucket where you are. . . . Cast it down in agriculture, mechanics, in commerce, in domestic service, and in the professions. . . . No race can prosper till it learns that there is as much dignity in tilling a field as in writing a poem. It is at the bottom of life we must begin, and not at the top."[3]

When they met in 1912, Walker expected Washington to see that she was an example of his own philosophy. She had started at the bottom and worked her way up to where she was now. As Walker watched for a chance to ask to speak at the NNBL meeting, someone else spoke up for her. George Knox, publisher of the Indianapolis newspaper *The Freeman*, requested that Madam Walker be allowed to address the convention. Washington appeared not to have heard Knox's request. He allowed someone else to speak. Walker was disappointed but not discouraged.

The following day, Walker waited patiently for the right moment to jump into the conversation. Then she bravely stood up and said loudly, "Surely, you are not going to shut the door in my face. I feel that I am in a business that is a credit to the womanhood of our race. I started in business seven years ago with only $1.50."[4]

When Walker saw that she had the attention of the audience, she continued with the story of how she had worked herself up from laundress to cook to president of her own company. Walker's short speech was a great success. Her goal was to let other businesspeople know that African-American women could succeed in business if they only recognized the opportunities that were right in front of them. Walker often liked to say, "The girls and women of our race must not be afraid to take hold of business endeavors . . . don't sit down and wait for the opportunities to come. . . . Get up and make them!"[5]

Walker also wanted the conference group to know that her company was offering African-American women the opportunity to gain financial independence. Walker's speech must have impressed Washington. He invited her to be one of the main speakers at the next NNBL convention, and she gladly accepted.

Although Walker was the sole stockowner of her company and would always be considered the company's best sales agent, her daughter, A'Lelia, had always played a major role in the company. A'Lelia Robinson, now twenty-eight years old, had been spending time in Harlem in New York City. The area was attracting African-American artists, writers, poets, and intellectuals. Robinson thought the Walker company should open a beauty shop in Harlem. In 1913, she persuaded her mother to buy a $90,000 townhouse on West 136th Street. When Walker saw the brownstone, which was built of Indiana limestone, she said, "A monument. . . . There is nothing to equal it, not even on Fifth Avenue."[6] Walker and her daughter converted the townhouse's lower level into a beauty parlor and school, and the upper level became private living quarters.

In 1916, Walker decided to make Harlem her home so she could be near her daughter and granddaughter. The Madam C. J. Walker Manufacturing Company headquarters, however, would remain in Indianapolis under the capable management of Ransom and Brokenburr. In Harlem, Walker became a popular and influential hostess, entertaining the best and brightest of the community.

She continued with her busy schedule. The

Walker used her wealth to help support a variety of African-American organizations. On the steps of Indianapolis's new black YMCA are, from left front, *Freeman* publisher George Knox, Madam Walker, Booker T. Washington, *Indianapolis World* publisher Alex Manning, and R. W. Bullock and Thomas Taylor of the YMCA. In the back row stand R. B. Ransom, left, and Walker's doctor, Colonel Joseph Ward.

demand for Walker products had increased to such an extent that she was now branching out to international markets in Central and South America and the Caribbean. By the fall of 1913, Walker had planned a trip to Jamaica, Cuba, Costa Rica, Haiti, and the Panama Canal Zone. The trip turned out to be a big success. Many women were eager to try her products as well as become Walker agents. These foreign markets increased Walker's sales and her growing number of beauty agents.

Walker's company now employed about twenty thousand agents in the United States, the Caribbean, and Central America. They worked out of their homes or in beauty salons, or were selling Walker hair products door-to-door. Walker agents could earn up to $25 a week, more than twice the typical salary of black women workers in the North. Southern black women were bringing home paychecks of only $2 per week for washing clothes and doing other manual labor. Many African-American women credited the Walker company with improving their lives. They had respect for their employer because she was truly one of them. Walker knew what it meant to work for a laundry-woman's earnings. Now she was showing hopeful and eager women that they could change their lives by becoming Walker beauty agents.

One Walker agent wrote Walker a letter saying, "You have opened up a trade for hundreds of colored women to make an honest and profitable living where they make as much in one week as a month's salary would bring from any other position that a colored woman can secure."[7]

There were now three Lelia beauty training colleges and hair parlors. One had opened in Pittsburgh in 1908; a second in Indianapolis in 1911; and a third in New York in 1913. They were training and graduating many successful businesspeople. One such person was Eva Cardel Lowery Bowman, who attended the Indianapolis school. Bowman eventually became the first African-American beauty inspector and examiner of cosmetology for the state of Tennessee. She also owned the Bowman Beauty and Barber College.[8]

Another successful Walker graduate was Marjorie Stewart Joyner. She had trained in a white beauty school and had tried her beauty school methods on her mother-in-law's hair. When these methods did not work on her thick, curly hair, Joyner's mother-in-law told her about Madam Walker's hair techniques. The younger Joyner took the Walker hair care course and opened her own Walker beauty salon in Chicago. She also recruited and trained Walker agents. Madam Walker rewarded Joyner by naming her national supervisor of the Lelia colleges and the Walker Beauty Schools.

In 1916, Walker decided to organize her agents into a union that would protect their rights as employees as well as create a feeling of togetherness. She initially called her union the National Beauty Culturists and Benevolent Association. The union benefits included a $50 death payment to each agent's beneficiary. The dues were 25 cents a month. Walker also formed local and state clubs for her agents and gave awards to outstanding agents with the most sales. In addition, she rewarded agents for their efforts at community service.

Meanwhile, Walker's granddaughter, Mae, was growing up. In September 1916 she entered Spelman Seminary in Atlanta, Georgia, to further her education. She was also being groomed for her future in the family business.

Toward the end of 1916, Walker began offering courses in her hair training methods to black colleges in the South. Mary McLeod Bethune, who had met Walker in 1912, added Walker's training to the course selection at her Daytona college.

While Walker was putting all of her time and energy into improving her employees' rights and benefits and into expanding her company, she was not paying attention to her own health. Although she was only forty-eight years old, Walker was suffering from high blood pressure. Her doctor advised her to reduce her workload, watch her diet, and ease up on travel. Walker was concerned enough to follow the doctor's orders, but before she took a rest, she wanted to visit

In this advertisement, Madam Walker promotes both her hair care products and the career opportunities for women who study "Madam C. J. Walker's System of Hair Culture."

her hometown of Delta, Louisiana. She went back to the Burney plantation, where she asked permission to visit the cabin that was her childhood home. Sarah Breedlove McWilliams Walker had come a long way from her humble beginnings. She was now considered America's richest African-American woman.

7

GIVING TO OTHERS

n November 1916, Walker was traveling through Mississippi when a terrible accident was narrowly avoided. As her car was crossing a railroad track, someone started shouting to get out of the way. When Walker turned around, she saw a freight train rushing toward them without any warning signals. Walker's driver stepped on the gas and sped forward. The car and its occupants had barely escaped injury. Walker was in such a state of nervous exhaustion after this near tragedy that she decided the time was right to follow the doctor's advice and take a much needed vacation.

Walker stayed at a health spa in Hot Springs, Arkansas, for more than two months. She bathed in the healing mineral waters of hot underground springs. These mineral waters were believed to bring relief to people suffering from arthritis and other medical problems. Walker also watched her diet, enjoyed body massages, and sipped herbal teas. Her goal was to regain her health and strength. Her daughter, A'Lelia, and factory forewoman Alice Kelly arrived to keep her company. Walker rested until February 1917, and by April she was back in New York City. She was ready to resume her many social, political, and business activities.

In 1917, the name of the Walker's employee union was changed to the Madam C. J. Walker Hair Culturists Union of America. The union's first annual national convention was held that year at the Philadelphia Union Baptist and Church Assembly Hall. More than two hundred Walker agents attended, proudly wearing Madam C. J. Walker membership ribbons.

Walker's keynote address to the members was titled "Women's Duty to Women." In her speech she advised the members "to remain loyal to our homes, our country and our flag."[1] She also made her agents aware that as independent women they were role models for other women. Madam Walker took an active role in the political and social issues of the times and encouraged her agents to become active as well.

Walker also advised and motivated her sales force. She stressed aggressive sales of her products by saying, "Hit often and hit hard. Strike with all your might."[2]

Madam Walker's success was evident in her fine clothes, expensive jewelry and cars, and beautiful homes. Yet in her rise to the top, she had not forgotten her difficult early life and the injustices African Americans had to live with on a daily basis. When Walker saw or heard about something that seemed

Madam Walker enjoyed driving around in her fashionable, modern automobile. Seated next to Walker is her niece Anjetta Breedlove. In the rear are factory forewoman Alice Kelly (behind Walker) and Walker's secretary, Lucy Flint.

unfair, she wanted to make it right. She once said, "My object in life is not simply to make money for myself or to spend it on myself in dressing or running around in an automobile, but I love to use a part of what I make in trying to help others."[3]

In the early twentieth century there were plenty of wrongs committed against African-American people. For example, in August 1906, Brownsville, Texas, had been the scene of a racial incident involving black soldiers stationed at nearby Fort Brown. At midnight on August 13, rifle shots on the streets killed one white citizen and wounded another. The chief of police was also injured. The black soldiers were accused of shooting up the town in response to ongoing harassment from the white population. Despite evidence of a frame-up, President Theodore Roosevelt dismissed the entire black regiment with a dishonorable discharge. He also disqualified the soldiers from further military or civil service. A Senate investigation supported Roosevelt's decision. A month later there was another riot in Atlanta, Georgia. Mobs of people attacked black citizens, killing twelve people and injuring seventy more.

Unfortunately, the number of violent racial incidents continued to grow as thousands of people fled from the southern states to the North. They hoped to escape from the prejudiced environment, beatings, and lynchings of the South. Northern whites, though, became angry when African Americans worked for low wages. The competition for jobs only added to the existing problems between the races.

In April 1917, the United States entered into World War I. America's war slogan was "Make the world safe for Democracy." African-American volunteers signed up at recruiting stations, ready to fight for their country. They were accepted into the U.S. Army and served in the infantry, medical corps, cavalry, ambulance corps, and many other branches. However, they were not allowed in the Marines, Air Force, and Coast Guard. The Navy accepted African Americans, but only as mess men. Their job was to prepare food in the kitchens. African-American servicemen were mistreated and segregated, even though they were entitled by law to the same rights as white Americans.

Because of the mistreatment of African Americans, there was much discussion among members of the African-American community about whether they should even fight for their country. Walker, like many other African-American leaders, believed that African Americans should go to war. She visited military training camps and encouraged African-American men to do their best for their country. Walker was hopeful that their participation in the war would help improve their social status. Perhaps they would get the respect and acceptance they deserved if white Americans saw that blacks were willing to give up their lives for their country.[4]

More than three hundred thousand African Americans served in the Armed Forces during World War I, although they fought in segregated units. Many of them received awards for bravery in action.

Meanwhile, riots and civil disturbances continued in the United States. An Arkansas riot in 1917 sent hundreds of African Americans to jail. On July 2, 1917, the worst race riot of all hit the city of East Saint Louis, Illinois. Thousands of African Americans fled from their burning homes. Hundreds of people were burned, beaten, and robbed. Many people died, and thousands lost their homes.[5]

Walker and other important African-American leaders were outraged at this violence. Madam Walker encouraged her agents to protest the murders of blacks across the country. "This is the greatest country under the sun," she told them. "But we must not let our love of country, our patriotic loyalty, cause us to abate one whit in our protest against wrong and injustice. We should protest until the American sense of justice is so aroused, that such affairs as the East St. Louis riot be forever impossible."[6]

On July 28, 1917, the National Association for the Advancement of Colored People and other equal rights activists organized the Negro Silent Protest Parade. Madam Walker was in the forefront as ten thousand to fifteen thousand African Americans silently marched down Manhattan's Fifth Avenue. People along the sidewalks were also silent. The only sounds were drum rolls and thousands of walking feet. African Americans' words and protests were written on signs carried by the protesters. Some of the signs read, "Thou Shalt Not Kill" and "Mr. President, why not make America safe for democracy?"[7]

The marchers also handed out pamphlets explaining the reasons for their protest:

> We march because we want to make impossible a repetition of Waco, Memphis, and East St. Louis by arousing the conscience of the country, and to bring the murderers of our brothers, sisters and innocent children to justice.
>
> We march because we deem it a crime to be silent in the face of such barbaric acts.
>
> We march because we are thoroughly opposed to Jim Crow cars, segregation, discrimination, disfranchisement, lynching, and the host of evils that are forced on us. . . .
>
> We march because we want our children to live in a better land and enjoy fairer conditions than have fallen to our lot.[8]

Walker and the other leaders decided the time was right to ask the president of the United States to make lynching a federal crime. They drew up a petition and scheduled an appointment with the president. They hoped that he would review their petition and then sign

Walker helped organize the Negro Silent Protest Parade in New York City in 1917. "We should protest until the American sense of justice is so aroused, that such affairs as the East St. Louis riot be forever impossible," said Madam Walker.

it. Walker and her group showed up at the White House on August 1, 1917, for their meeting. They were turned away. President Woodrow Wilson's secretary told them that the president was busy and could not keep his appointment with them. Walker and the others left, but not before handing the petition to the secretary.

Walker was disappointed with the president's lack of interest in their petition. However, she still had hopes that Congress would pass an antilynching bill.

She kept on voicing her concerns and urged Congress to continue to look into the injustices directed against African-American people.

Only a month after the silent protest march in New York City, a riot erupted in Houston, Texas. The men of the Twenty-fourth Infantry Battalion were tired of being brutally treated by white officers and civilians. When African-American soldiers went into town from their camp outside Houston, they were arrested. Eventually, a fight erupted and seventeen white people were killed. Sixty-three African-American soldiers were court-martialed, and thirteen were sentenced to hang, without right of appeal. Forty-one were sent to prison for life.

Walker could not prevent these racial problems, but she did use her influence and money to support her social and political views. She spoke out against lynchings, and she traveled around the country to help raise money for the National Association for the Advancement of Colored People.

In her travels, Walker met a variety of interesting and influential people. Many were African-American women who had come from similar economic and social backgrounds and worked passionately for their beliefs. One of them was Ida B. Wells-Barnett, a brave journalist whom Walker had come to know through the fight against the lynching of African Americans.

Wells-Barnett was an educator, editor, journalist,

and political activist. She was also a fierce crusader committed to identifying and punishing lynchers. Barnett was five years older than Walker and had been born in Mississippi. At the age of sixteen, she lost her parents to yellow fever. Like Walker, Wells-Barnett was orphaned and had to take on grown-up responsibilities at an early age. Wells-Barnett had to become a parent to her five younger brothers and sisters.

Walker and Wells-Barnett both worked for civil rights and social change. While Walker was building her company and offering many women the opportunity to pull themselves out of poverty, Wells-Barnett had joined the National Equal Rights League and became chairperson of the Anti-lynching Bureau of the National Afro-American Council. When three of her friends were brutally murdered in a lynching, Wells-Barnett was outraged and wrote editorials in her paper, the Memphis *Free Speech and Headlight*. She then began to investigate and document this violence by visiting the sites of lynchings, reading newspaper reports, and interviewing eyewitnesses. She documented more than seven hundred lynchings during a ten-year period.

In 1892, Wells-Barnett had published a report on lynchings called *The Red Record*. She paid a price for her outspokenness. Her newspaper office was burned and destroyed. In addition, she was banned from the South and was threatened with bodily harm if she returned. She took up residence in New York City, but her exile from the South did not stop her from expressing her views. In June 1892, *The New York Age*, an African-American newspaper, printed an article she wrote with names, dates, and places of hundreds of lynchings. Later, her findings were printed in a booklet, "Southern Horror: Lynch Law in All Its Phases."[9]

African-American women did not forget Wells-Barnett's hard work to abolish lynching. They rallied around her in her struggle. Walker was one of her strongest supporters. She respected Wells-Barnett's dedication and activism and supported her politically and financially in any way she could.

Walker also channeled her energy and financial resources to support education. Walker had a thirst for knowledge and a strong respect for people who devoted their lives to educating young people. The statistics on educational opportunities for African-American children were startling. In the early 1900s in Atlanta, Georgia, African-American children attended school only three and a half hours a day.[10] Over the years, most of those responsible for providing schools and an education for African-American children living in the southern states were African-American women. Many of these women built their own schools, provided their own supplies, and had to continually raise funds to keep their schools open.

Walker was proud of the gains made in educating

black children. She rewarded these educational pioneers by giving their schools cash donations and funding educational scholarships.

The list of Walker's charitable donations is impressive. She gave generously to the Scholarship Fund for Young Women at Tuskegee Institute. She gave $5,000 to the Daytona Normal and Industrial Institute for Negro Girls, and an equal amount to Lucy Laney's Haines Institute in Augusta, Georgia. She supported other causes as well. She gave money to the Young Men's Christian Association of Indianapolis, and made many contributions to the National Association for the Advancement of Colored People.

One of the schools that benefited greatly from Walker's generosity was the Alice Freeman Palmer Memorial Institute. This private secondary school for African Americans was located in Sedalia, North Carolina. The institute was founded in 1902 by Charlotte Hawkins Brown, an African-American educator born in Henderson, North Carolina.

Charlotte Hawkins Brown, like Madam Walker, was not afraid to go after her dreams. Early in life, she showed a talent for public speaking and leadership. She was also artistically gifted and drew portraits of her fellow students. She graduated from high school in 1900, just a few years before Walker went into the hair care business. At the age of eighteen, Hawkins left the State Normal School in Salem, Massachusetts, one year before graduation to accept a job as a teacher in Sedalia, North Carolina.

On October 12, 1901, Hawkins held her first class for fifty children at the Bethany Institute, a small school located in the Bethany Congregational Church. Her monthly salary was $30, but she spent most of it on clothes and school supplies for the children. After a year, the school closed for lack of funds. Hawkins was offered a job elsewhere, but she was committed to the community of Sedalia. Besides, she dreamed of building a school, and like Walker she was intent upon making her dream a reality.

On October 10, 1902, Hawkins, just nineteen years old, succeeded in opening her own school. She named it the Alice Freeman Palmer Institute in honor of a friend and educator who had paid for Hawkins's education. She later changed the name to the Alice Freeman Palmer Memorial Institute. Hawkins went on to become deeply involved in the fight for civil rights for African Americans. She helped found the National Council of Negro Women and other organizations and spoke out passionately against lynching and in support of equality among the races.

When Madam Walker heard about a worthy project, she did not hesitate to add her support. The National Association of Colored Women took up the cause of saving the home of the late Frederick Douglass, the devoted abolitionist and advocate of women's rights and world peace. Douglass was born a slave in 1817 and escaped to the North in 1838 when he was twenty-one years old. He dedicated his life to helping runaway slaves and to ending slavery. He stated in his newspaper, the *North Star*, that his goals were "to abolish slavery in all its forms" and to promote "UNIVERSAL EMANCIPATION."[11] Frederick Douglass, who died in 1895, is often called the foremost African-American leader of the nineteenth century.

Douglass's house in Anacostia, a neighborhood in Washington, D.C., was to open as a museum and historical center operated by the Frederick Douglass Memorial and Historical Association. However, there was still an unpaid mortgage of $5,000, a sum the association was not able to pay. The NACW did not want to see this valuable piece of history lost, so it began a fund-raising campaign to rescue the home. After two years, the mortgage was paid off, and another $30,000 was raised to improve the house and property. Walker's $500 donation was the largest individual contribution made to save the Douglass home.

Back in 1916, Walker had purchased additional real estate of her own—four and a half acres of land just north of New York City. Her property overlooked the Hudson River in the well-to-do community of Irvington-on-Hudson. There, her mansion was nearing completion. Walker's neighbors included the wealthy John D. Rockefeller and the famous Tiffany family. The house was so large and grand that her friend Ida Wells-Barnett once asked her what she would do with its thirty rooms. Walker answered, "I want plenty of room in which to entertain my friends. I have worked so hard all my life that I would like to rest."[12]

An article appeared in *The New York Times* in 1917 with the title "Wealthiest Negro Woman's Suburban Mansion: Estate at Irvington, Overlooking Hudson and Containing All the Attractions That a Big Fortune Commands."[13]

When Walker drove up in her small electric car to inspect her property, she attracted lots of attention.

Madam Walker built a luxurious mansion overlooking the Hudson River. The estate featured "all the attractions that a big fortune commands," announced an article in *The New York Times.*

Would her white neighbors accept this African-American woman into their exclusive neighborhood? Eventually, the residents of Irvington Village came to realize that their new neighbor was a thoughtful, quiet, and respected woman who had worked very hard for her success. This African-American entrepreneur was a role model for all races.

Walker's plan was to retire to her New York mansion. She wanted to spend more time with her daughter and granddaughter. But she still kept up her busy pace, even though her doctor kept telling her to slow down and take care of her health. When her blood pressure soared, she was finally forced to cut back on her work and social engagements. Her physician told her to watch her diet by eliminating salt and fatty foods. She also had to exercise more and limit her daily schedule. If she did not follow these suggestions, he warned, her high blood pressure could lead to a stroke, heart problems, or kidney disease.

Walker's doctor told her to check in at the Kellogg Medical Clinic in Battle Creek, Michigan, for an evaluation and treatment program. For years, Walker had pushed herself time and time again beyond her physical limits. To achieve her goals, she had ignored her own health. But now, she had to put herself first. Walker had no other choice than to follow her doctor's orders.

8

VILLA LEWARO

Walker's large, cream-colored two-story Italian Renaissance–style home in Irvington-on-Hudson was designed by an African-American architect named Vertner Woodson Tandy. The cost was estimated to be close to $250,000.[1] Tandy, who also designed Walker's New York City townhouse, was the first black architect registered in New York State.

In early 1918, Walker was waiting to move into her new estate. She knew she should be following medical advice and limiting her activities. But as usual, there was always another trip planned, another speaking engagement. As soon as she was released from the

Battle Creek Clinic, she traveled to Des Moines, Iowa, where she was the keynote speaker at a National Association for the Advancement of Colored People fund-raiser for its antilynching campaign. After the NAACP appearance, Walker continued on an extended tour throughout the Midwest and East to raise more money for the NAACP.

Finally, in June 1918, Madam Walker settled down to live in her new home. She named the estate Villa Lewaro, a name created by Enrico Caruso, a family friend and a famous opera singer of the time. He combined the first two syllables of each word of Walker's daughter's name, A'*Le*lia *Wa*lker *Ro*binson, to form the acronym Lewaro.

Walker was content to stay home and work in her garden or put the finishing touches on her new house. Villa Lewaro had thirty rooms. A white marble staircase led to the second floor, where Walker's bedroom was located. The bedroom had a large four-poster bed with a red velvet canopy. The estate also included a gym with showers, a library filled with hundreds of books, a conservatory, a pool room, vaults for valuables, and a chapel. The grounds were also spectacular, planted with gingko trees, copper beeches, and outdoor gardens. Walker spent many peaceful hours planting rose bushes and tending her vegetable garden.

Walker in a quiet moment in her New York mansion. "I have worked so hard all my life that I would like to rest," said Walker—but she rarely slowed down her busy schedule.

The interior decoration of the mansion cost almost half a million dollars. The furnishings included an expensive dining room suite, a piano trimmed with 24-carat gold, and a pipe organ. Walker placed colorful Persian rugs on the floors and costly oil paintings on the walls. Marble and bronze statuettes stood in glass cabinets and on tables and ledges throughout the house.

Villa Lewaro was a wonderful place, but the costs of

building and maintaining the estate put a strain on Walker's finances. She now had a large monthly mortgage payment. In addition, she would have to make payments on some of the interior furnishings for several years. Still, although her living expenses were high, Walker was proud that she could show other people, both white and black, what an African American could achieve with hard work and determination. Madam Walker saw herself as a role model. She built Villa Lewaro as an example and inspiration for other African Americans. She wanted them "to see what could be accomplished, no matter what their background."[2]

In the middle of that first summer in Villa Lewaro, Walker was invited to Denver for the annual convention of the National Association of Colored Women. She was to be honored there for making the largest personal contribution toward paying off the mortgage on the historic home of black abolitionist Frederick Douglass. It was a proud moment for Walker when she was invited to hold a lighted candle to the paid-up mortgage document.

When she returned to Villa Lewaro, Walker began planning a celebration to officially open her dream house. She wanted to use the occasion to pay tribute to her guest of honor, Emmett J. Scott, in his new position as special assistant to the secretary of war in charge of Negro affairs in President Woodrow Wilson's

A gathering of Walker agents in front of Villa Lewaro. Walker built the mansion to inspire other African Americans to "see what could be accomplished, no matter what their background."

administration. Walker invited many important politicians, NAACP leaders, ministers, and educators to the party. Their attendance was certain to promote interesting conversation. One of the most talked about issues of the time was the upcoming return of African-American soldiers from World War I. It was hoped that the social status of the black veterans would improve because of their participation in the war.

Walker continued to open her beautiful home for many social and political gatherings. She had taken great care in decorating her mansion, and she enjoyed sharing it with other people. On December 23, 1918, Walker celebrated her fifty-first birthday surrounded by family and friends. On Christmas, there were many activities going on at Villa Lewaro—a festive dinner, the unwrapping of presents, holiday carols, and just relaxing. It was a warm and friendly time, as observed by Walker's friend Hallie Queen. She wrote, "So ended . . . Christmas . . . and it was impressed upon my mind a memory of her goodness, devotion, reverence, humility, and faith."[3]

Walker was looking forward to the new year. She

Madam Walker's beauty culturists fill the many staircases and walkways surrounding the fountain behind Villa Lewaro. Walker entertained lavishly—and often—at her grand mansion.

was planning to spend more time at Villa Lewaro, but she was also working on a new line of skin care products. Unfortunately, her health was not improving. Her blood pressure had continued to rise, putting more strain on her already weakened kidneys. Her doctor, Colonel Joseph Ward, ordered her to stay close to home. For a while, Walker obeyed his orders and spent her time quietly. She wrote letters to family and friends and gave small dinner parties.

On November 11, 1918, World War I ended. A conference was to be held in Versailles, near Paris, to draw up the peace settlement. The conference involved negotiations between Germany, Great Britain, France, Italy, Japan, and the United States. African Americans worried that the negotiations would not recognize the needs of African Americans or of blacks in Africa. They decided to hold their own meeting in Paris to coincide with the Versailles Peace Conference. This Pan-African Congress was organized by W. E. B. Du Bois, the noted African-American scholar and activist.

Another African-American leader, Monroe Trotter, also planned a meeting in Paris. Trotter had founded the National Equal Rights League (NERL). Walker and Wells-Barnett were two of the eleven delegates selected to attend the Paris talks on behalf of the NERL. Some people in Walker's company expressed concern that her attendance at this conference could jeopardize her business if the NERL became too radical. As it turned out, Trotter was denied a passport and the NERL delegates did not go to Paris.

W. E. B. Du Bois did present his congress's views to the Versailles Peace Conference. However, the final document, the Treaty of Versailles, signed in June 1919, did not include a pledge for equal rights for Africans and their descendants throughout the world. Walker was disappointed during this difficult period, but she continued to devote time to many other related projects and concerns.

In April 1919, Walker decided to go to St. Louis to publicize her new products. While she was staying with a friend, her physical condition worsened. She returned to New York in a private railroad car. Her doctor came to her home to examine her. He found that she was suffering from acute kidney failure caused by years of high blood pressure. After getting over the shock of the diagnosis, Walker immediately began to donate large sums of money to various organizations. She knew that her illness was life-threatening, and she wanted to ensure her support for the NAACP and other important institutions and causes. She gave a total of $25,000 to a variety of African-American organizations.

Walker's spirits improved when she received a surprise letter from her daughter, who was on a business trip in South America. Throughout the years, Walker and A'Lelia had not always agreed on A'Lelia's choice of men. Now, in her letter, A'Lelia informed her mother that she had decided to marry Dr. James Arthur Kennedy. Even though she had doubts about the relationship with Kennedy, A'Lelia wanted to please her mother, who was in poor health.[4]

On May 16, 1919, Walker wrote what turned out to be her final letter to her daughter. It read, in part:

My Darling Baby:

Lou and Edna just read me your letters and you made me very happy to know that at last you have decided to marry Kennedy. Although I have never let you know this, it has been my wish ever since I met Wylie in Wash. I never thought he would make you happy, but I do believe Kennedy will. . . . Nettie and the girls join me in love to you and Mae and I send with my love, kisses and kisses and kisses.

Your Devoted,
Mother[5]

Soon after writing this letter, Madam C. J. Walker fell into a coma. She died on May 25, 1919. She was only fifty-one years old.

When A'Lelia Walker Robinson was notified of her mother's death, she hurried home with her daughter, Mae. They arrived just in time to join the one thousand mourners—friends, family, and business acquaintances—who attended the funeral services at Villa Lewaro.

On June 3, 1919, Walker was buried in New York's

Woodlawn Cemetery. Mary McLeod Bethune paid a fitting tribute to her friend when she said, "She was the clearest demonstration I know of Negro woman's ability recorded in history. She has gone, but her work still lives as an inspiration not only to her race, but to the world."[6]

9

A'LELIA AND THE WALKER COMPANY

Before her death, Madam Walker had written to her company manager that she was not, in fact, a millionaire as everyone thought. Only three years after she died, her holdings, properties, and overall wealth amounted to $509,863, more than half a million dollars. Her stocks and bonds, including her holdings in the Walker company, were valued at $212,309. Her real estate (subject to mortgages of $120,000) was worth $247,424. Mortgages, notes, and bonds came to another $20,062, and jewelry and household goods amounted to $30,068.[1]

Walker was a wealthy woman who enjoyed spending

money. She had large business and personal expenses, yet she always managed to share her wealth with others, even after her death. Her will was divided into four parts. Most of her property, including Villa Lewaro and a one-third interest in the Walker company, was left to her only child, A'Lelia. The second part of the will gave the remaining two thirds of the company to five trustees, including A'Lelia Robinson and Freeman Ransom, her general manager. The third part included contributions to many schools and organizations, such as the Tuskegee Institute and YMCA's located in cities around the country. The last part listed gifts of personal property and money to relatives, friends, and employees.

In addition to her many bequests, Walker also included another important item in her will. She wanted her company always to be headed by a woman.[2] Walker's daughter, A'Lelia Walker Robinson, became the president of the company, and Freeman Ransom retained his position as general manager. He was also responsible for giving out funds to the various charities named in Walker's will and for the maintenance of Villa Lewaro.

Working together, Walker and her daughter had helped many African-American women to have pride in their appearance. A'Lelia Walker herself was an example of this effort. She had healthy, thick, wavy hair that she liked to adorn with dazzling turbans. She was almost six feet tall and carried herself in a regal manner.

The two Walker women respected and loved each other, but they had not always shared the same opinions. A friend once described them as "fire and ice."[3]

At the time of her mother's death, A'Lelia Walker Robinson was almost thirty-four years old and engaged to Dr. Kennedy, as she had written in a letter to her mother. However, three days after her mother's funeral, she followed her heart and married another man instead. Dr. Wiley Wilson was the man she really loved, despite her mother's disapproval. Unfortunately, this marriage did not last, and Robinson escaped from her marital problems by taking a long overseas trip. While on this trip, she began to renew her romance with Dr. Kennedy through a series of letters.

During this time of personal problems, A'Lelia Walker Wilson maintained an active interest in the family business. Still, she preferred to leave the day-to-day operation of the company to Freeman Ransom and the other trusted employees her mother had hired. The company was doing so well by the mid-1920s that she was free of company worries and had plenty of time to travel and entertain friends.

A'Lelia Walker also became a minor celebrity in the Harlem Renaissance. The Harlem Renaissance was a blossoming of the arts in the African-American community. In this thriving cultural movement, art and literature expressed the experience of being black in America. Blacks and whites alike read books and poetry by African-American writers and intellectuals, listened to jazz and blues, and applauded all-black theater.

A'Lelia Walker was caught up in the excitement. She became acquainted with the stars of the Harlem Renaissance—poets and writers such as Countee Cullen, James Weldon Johnson, W. E. B. Du Bois, Zora Neale Hurston, and Langston Hughes. She supported the arts both socially and financially. Poet Langston Hughes paid her a compliment by calling her "Joy Goddess" of the Harlem Renaissance because she liked to entertain and bring interesting and creative people together.[4]

In 1923, Madam Walker's adopted granddaughter, Mae, married Dr. Gordon Jackson of Chicago. A'Lelia Walker Wilson planned an expensive wedding for her daughter at Saint Philips Episcopal Church in Harlem. A few years later, in 1926, A'Lelia Walker had her own wedding. After her divorce from her second husband, Dr. Wiley Wilson, she married Dr. James A. Kennedy, the man her mother had wanted her to marry seven years earlier.

A'Lelia Walker Kennedy now had three homes: the New York City townhouse in Harlem on 136th Street, a newly purchased apartment at 80 Edgecombe Avenue, and Villa Lewaro. She spent most of her time

Madam Walker's glamorous daughter, A'Lelia, hosted parties for the artists and writers who were the celebrities of the Harlem Renaissance.

in Harlem, but she also liked to give large parties at the mansion in Irvington-on-Hudson.

In 1927, A'Lelia Walker Kennedy decided to offer her townhouse as a meeting place to nurture and promote the talents of artists, writers, painters, musicians, philosophers, and educators. At the time, this kind of gathering place was called a salon. Walker Kennedy's salon was decorated in strong colors of red and gold. It became known as the "Dark Tower," after a column in *Opportunity* magazine written by the well-known African-American poet Countee Cullen. Walker Kennedy offered food, drink, and beautiful surroundings. She often played bridge while her guests enjoyed refreshments and lively conversation.

Walker Kennedy was well known for her lavish parties. She was considered an important hostess because she provided a gathering place for so many brilliant people. However, not everyone was impressed with her wealth and parties. Some artists resented her involvement in the Harlem Renaissance movement because she was neither an intellectual nor a literary critic. She was sometimes thought of as a poor little rich girl trying to climb the ladder of social acceptance—after all, she was the daughter of a former laundress. Without her mother's wealth, some thought, Walker Kennedy would not have received such recognition. For most black writers, however, A'Lelia Walker's patronage was essential and greatly appreciated.[5]

Walker Kennedy, with her one-third interest in the Walker company, continued to plan improvements. In 1927, she had a new factory headquarters built at the corner of West Street and Indiana Avenue in Indianapolis. The location was ideal. Indiana Avenue was the heart of the city, populated with schools, churches, and African-American-owned businesses. Walker Manufacturing's $350,000 new building was a blocklong office and professional complex that included a beauty shop, drugstore, and coffee shop as well as a 944-seat theater and a casino/ballroom large enough to accommodate 350 people. It served as a cultural center for the African-American community. Today, it is registered as a state historical landmark and is listed on the National Register of Historic Places. The building was once described as a "city within a building."[6]

In 1929, the stock market crashed and the United States soon began to experience severe economic problems. This time in history is known as the Great Depression. Millions of people were out of work, and they certainly could not afford luxuries like beauty products. The Walker company's sales dropped sharply. The high expenses of maintaining Villa Lewaro, Walker Kennedy's Harlem townhouse, and her expensive lifestyle, combined with a weak economy, caused the closing of several Walker beauty parlors.

In 1931, after five years of marriage, A'Lelia Walker Kennedy's private life was once again in trouble. She

The Madam C. J. Walker Manufacturing Company—"a city within a building"—took up an entire block in Indianapolis. It included professional offices, a movie theater, a ballroom, and shops.

and her husband had different interests and schedules. They saw little of each other, and this separation caused a gradual breakdown of the marriage. Walker Kennedy decided it was time to divorce her husband. A few months after this decision, she died suddenly after suffering a stroke at a friend's house in Long Branch, New Jersey. She was only forty-six years old.

The Reverend Adam Clayton Powell, Sr., spoke fondly about her at the funeral services. Langston Hughes remembered her in a poem entitled "To A'Lelia." Singers who had performed at Walker Kennedy's parties sang Noel Coward's song "I'll See

You Again." Then Walker beauty agents who had gathered from around the country brought flowers and placed them on the bier—the platform on which her coffin rested. Mary McLeod Bethune spoke about her friend Madam C. J. Walker and how she had worked to build up a successful business and then had given it to her daughter.[7]

Although the two Walker women were now gone, the Madam C. J. Walker Manufacturing Company was still in business. According to the terms of Walker's will, another woman would head the company. Madam C. J. Walker's adopted granddaughter, Mae, now married to Marion Perry, was destined to be the new president.

10

THE MEMORY AND LEGACY OF MADAM C. J. WALKER

After A'Lelia Walker Kennedy's death in 1931, Mae Walker Perry inherited her mother's share of the company stock. The remaining shares belonged to Freeman Ransom, the trusted financial manager of the company. Walker Kennedy also willed Villa Lewaro to the National Association for the Advancement of Colored People. A year later, it was sold for $50,000 to Companions of the Forest, a white women's group that used it as a retirement home for several years. The Harlem townhouse at 136th Street, which had been home to Walker Kennedy's famous salon, the Dark Tower, was leased to New York City to protect Walker's property from creditors.

Mae Walker Perry took an active interest in the company. She ran the business along with Freeman Ransom. When Walker Perry died in 1945, A'Lelia Mae Perry—her daughter from her second marriage, and Madam Walker's great-granddaughter—inherited the Walker company stock. A'Lelia Mae Perry was a student at Howard University, but she became president of the Walker company for a short time. However, she was forced to give up this position because of a family disagreement and a lawsuit filed by her father, Marion Perry. After the lawsuit was settled, A'Lelia Mae Perry accepted a position as vice president. She married S. Henry Bundles and had three children. She stayed active in the company until her death in 1976.

Walker company products had grown to include toothpaste, face powder, cold cream, rouge, bath oil and powder, perfume, and deodorant. A hair conditioner called Satin Tress had been developed by Marjorie Joyner, supervisor of the Walker Beauty Schools. The products continued to be sold by Walker agents, as well as through a company called Kiefer-Stewart. Sales were still good, but by 1979, net sales were down to less than $100,000 a year.

By the 1980s, the African-American hair care business had grown into a $2 billion market, according to the American Health and Beauty Aids Institute.[1]

There was now plenty of competition for the Walker company, which had been serving the hair care needs of African-American women for more than seventy-five years.

In 1985, the company's manufacturing branch was sold to Ray Randolph, an Indianapolis businessman. The purchase price was undisclosed. At the Walker property at 617 Indiana Avenue in Indianapolis, the Walker theater was in need of repair, and it became a $3.5 million seven-year project of the Madame C. J. Walker Urban Life Center.

On October 14, 1988, there was a celebration for the reopening of the Madam Walker Theatre. Many well-known people showed up for the ceremonies. Gregory Hines, the Broadway and movie actor and dancer; Alex Haley, author of the book *Roots*; and actor Roscoe Lee Brown, who played Gordon on *Sesame Street*, attended the celebration. Most important, two of Madam Walker's great-great-grandchildren, Mark Bundles and A'Lelia Perry Bundles, were present.[2] The revitalized Walker complex includes professional offices, a cultural center for the community, and the Madame Walker Heritage Center. Today the center operates under a mission "dedicated to nurturing and celebrating the arts from an African-American perspective."[3]

A'Lelia Perry Bundles and her brothers, Mark and Lance, have worked hard to preserve their great-great-grandmother's memory for the African-American community. A'Lelia Bundles, in particular, has taken a special interest in telling the story of Madam C. J. Walker's life. Bundles, a network television news producer for more than twenty years, is deputy bureau chief for *ABC News* in Washington, D.C. She has written extensively about Madam C. J. Walker.

Bundles's admiration for her great-great-grandmother is evident: "She had to strike out on her own at a very young age. She had to grow up very fast. She had to become independent. That kind of independence often creates a perseverance and a strength and a courage that other people are not called upon to make at such an early point in their lives."[4]

In an article titled "A Letter to My Great-Great-Grandmother, Madam C. J. Walker," Bundles explained her feelings in more detail:

> I know we've never met, but I've known about you for as long as I can remember. Our attic was filled with treasures from Villa Lewaro, your mansion in Irvington, New York. . . .
>
> As a child, I entertained myself for entire Sunday afternoons exploring your old brown leather trunk, each new compartment more breath-taking than the last. A small lacquered compact of Mme. C. J. Walker's Egyptian Tan Powder tucked here. A monogrammed hair clip hidden there. Miniature mummy charms from Cairo here. . . .
>
> There is so much more I'd love to tell you. But, for now, just know that I feel blessed to have you as my

Today, A'Lelia Perry Bundles, above, is dedicated to preserving the memory of her great-great-grandmother, Madam C. J. Walker.

great-great-grandmother and grateful that I am able to share your good deeds with others.

Lovingly,
A'Lelia[5]

In a speech, Bundles once said, "What I love most about sharing the story of Madam's life is that it reminds me that we as black women have been blazing trails for many, many years. Our foremothers were so determined and so creative. It lets me know we don't have the luxury of giving up."[6]

In 1993, another piece of Madam Walker's life history and legacy was preserved. Villa Lewaro, her beloved home, was purchased by Harold E. Doley, Jr. A successful businessman, Doley is the first African American to have a membership on the New York Stock Exchange. He bought Villa Lewaro from a white couple that had owned it for many years.

Doley said, "There's only been one home that I've ever wanted to own and this is it. Madam Walker said she wanted this home to represent what is doable in America by people of African descent."[7] Doley dedicated himself to repairing Villa Lewaro, which had fallen into disrepair. In 1995, Villa Lewaro's renovations were completed. "Restoring the mansion to its previous grandeur has been no small feat," said Doley.[8]

A'Lelia Bundles was pleased with the villa's restoration. She commented that Doley understood the importance of the mansion by creating the same atmosphere in the house that Madam Walker intended.[9] Bundles proudly remembered visiting Villa Lewaro. She wrote as though she were speaking to her great-great-grandmother: "I was overwhelmed with pride as I imagined you presiding over elegant social gatherings and hosting meetings of the 'race leaders' of your day."[10]

Even after her death, Madam C. J. Walker has received honors for her business success. She is included in the United States National Hall of Fame, where she is recognized as the only African-American woman to receive such a distinction. On January 28, 1998, a United States postage stamp was issued to honor the achievements of this remarkable woman. Her stamp is number twenty-one in the Black Heritage Commemorative Series and features a portrait of Walker taken by Washington photographer Addison Scurlock.

Madam C. J. Walker's memory and legacy continue to be an example of what determination and self-sacrifice can bring to those who are willing to say to themselves, as she once said, "There is no royal flower-strewn road to success. And if there is, I have not found it, for if I have accomplished anything in life it is because I have been willing to work hard."[11]

CHRONOLOGY

1867—Sarah Breedlove is born on December 23 in Delta, Louisiana.

1874—Sarah's mother and father die.

1878—Sarah and her sister move to Vicksburg, Mississippi, and find work as washerwomen.

1882—Sarah marries Moses (Jeff) McWilliams.

1885—Gives birth to a daughter, Lelia, on June 6.

1887—Husband dies.

1888—Sarah McWilliams moves to St. Louis, Missouri.

1904—At the St. Louis World's Fair, is inspired by Margaret Murray Washington's speech.

1905—Dreams about a hair formula; moves to Denver, Colorado, where she begins to develop and sell hair care products.

1906—Marries Charles Joseph Walker on January 4; begins a sales promotion tour around the country as Madam C. J. Walker.

1908—Hires Walker agents to sell her products; moves to Pittsburgh, Pennsylvania; opens Lelia College to train Walker hair culturists.

1910—Moves to Indianapolis, Indiana; opens new Walker company headquarters.

1911—Legally incorporates the Walker company; builds larger headquarters that even include a movie theater.

1912—Divorces Charles Walker; daughter adopts Mae Bryant; Walker attends the National Negro Business League convention to speak about her hair care business.

1913—Buys a townhouse for her daughter in Harlem, New York City.

1916—Organizes her agents into a union; moves from Indianapolis to New York City.

1917—On July 28, attends the Negro Silent Protest Parade against the East Saint Louis, Illinois, race riot; in August, holds first annual national union convention in Philadelphia.

1918—Moves into her new Irvington-on-Hudson mansion called Villa Lewaro.

1919—Becomes ill at a friend's home in St. Louis; dies on May 25; A'Lelia inherits most of her mother's fortune.

CHAPTER NOTES

Chapter 1. Sarah's Vision

1. Darlene Clark Hine and Kathleen Thompson, *A Shining Thread of Hope: The History of Black Women in America* (New York: Broadway Books, 1998), p. 204.

2. Marion W. Taylor, *Madam C. J. Walker, Pioneer Businesswoman* (New York: Chelsea House Publishers, 1994), p. 31.

3. Gene N. Landrum, *Profiles of Black Success: Thirteen Creative Geniuses Who Changed the World* (New York: Prometheus Books, 1997), p. 28.

4. Darlene Clark Hine, *Black Women in America, An Historical Encyclopedia* (Bloomington: Indiana University Press, 1994), vol. 2, p. 1209.

Chapter 2. The Almost-Christmas Baby

1. Dorothy Hoobler and Thomas Hoobler, *The African-American Family Album* (New York: Oxford University Press, 1995), p. 51.

2. Note to the author from A'Lelia Perry Bundles, January 13, 1999.

3. A'Lelia Perry Bundles, *Madam C. J. Walker, Entrepreneur* (New York: Chelsea House Publishers, 1991), pp. 22–23.

4. Jessie Carney Smith, *Black Heroes of the 20th Century* (Detroit: Visible Ink Press, 1998), p. 625.

Chapter 3. A Home of Her Own

1. Mitchell C. Brown, *Madam C. J. Walker: Inventor, Business-Woman* (Louisiana State University Libraries, December 13, 1996), p. 1.

2. Jim Haskins, *One More River to Cross: The Stories of Twelve Black Americans* (New York: Scholastic Inc., 1992), p. 17.

3. Note to the author from A'Lelia Perry Bundles, January 13, 1999.

4. A'Lelia Perry Bundles, *Madam C. J. Walker, Entrepreneur* (New York: Chelsea House Publishers, 1991), p. 27.

5. Ibid., pp. 31–32.

6. A'Lelia Bundles, "Madam C. J. Walker," *American History*, August 1996, p. 45.

Chapter 4. Sarah's Invention

1. Jessie Carney Smith, *Black Heroes of the 20th Century* (Detroit: Visible Ink Press, 1998), p. 626.

2. A'Lelia Perry Bundles, *Madam C. J. Walker, Entrepreneur* (New York: Chelsea House Publishers, 1991), p. 37.

3. "Madam C. J. Walker: Hairdresser, entrepreneur, and educational counselor," *DISCovering U.S. History on GaleNet*, 1999, <http://wale.gale.com/markets/schools/resrcs/womenhst/walkercj.htm> (February 25, 1999).

4. Schlessinger Productions, *The Black Americans of Achievement Video Collection; Madam C. J. Walker* (Bala Cynwyd, Pa., 1992).

5. Jessie Carney Smith, *Notable Black American Women* (Detroit: Gale Research Inc., 1992), p. 1187.

6. Smith, *Black Heroes of the 20th Century*, p. 628.

7. Nathan Aaseng, *Black Inventors* (New York: Facts on File, 1997), p. 83.

8. A'Lelia Bundles, "Madam C. J. Walker," *American History*, August 1996, pp. 46–47.

Chapter 5. A Family Business

1. Carol DeKane Nagel, ed., *African American Biography* (Detroit: Gale Research, Inc. 1994), vol. 4, p. 750.

⊡⊡⊡⊡⊡⊡⊡⊡⊡⊡⊡⊡⊡⊡⊡⊡⊡⊡⊡⊡⊡⊡⊡⊡⊡⊡⊡⊡⊡⊡⊡⊡⊡⊡⊡⊡

2. Cookie Lommel, *Madam C. J. Walker, Entrepreneur* (Los Angeles: Melrose Square Publishing Company, 1993), p. 155.

3. A'Lelia Bundles, "Lost Women: Madam C. J. Walker—Cosmetics Tycoon," *Ms.*, July 1983, p. 93.

4. Darlene Clark Hine, ed., *Black Women in America, An Historical Encyclopedia* (Bloomington: Indiana University Press, 1994), vol. 2, p. 1209.

5. Jim Haskins, *One More River to Cross: The Stories of Twelve Black Americans* (New York: Scholastic, Inc., 1992), p. 19.

Chapter 6. Growing Bigger and Better

1. Jim Haskins, *One More River to Cross: The Stories of Twelve Black Americans* (New York: Scholastic, Inc., 1992), p. 20.

2. Cookie Lommel, *Madam C. J. Walker, Entrepreneur* (Los Angeles: Melrose Square Publishing Company, 1993), p. 94.

3. Dorothy Hoobler and Thomas Hoobler, *The African-American Family Album* (New York: Oxford University Press, 1995), p. 64.

4. A'Lelia Perry Bundles, *Madam C. J. Walker, Entrepreneur* (New York: Chelsea House Publishers, 1991), p. 13.

5. Darlene Clark Hine and Kathleen Thompson, *A Shining Thread of Hope: The History of Black Women in America* (New York: Broadway Books, 1998), p. 204.

6. Darlene Clark Hine, ed., "Madam C. J. Walker (Sarah Breedlove) (1867–1919)," *Black Women in America, An Historical Encyclopedia* (Bloomington: Indiana University Press, 1994), vol. 2, pp. 1211–1212.

7. A'Lelia Bundles, "America's First Self-Made Woman Millionaire," *Radcliffe Quarterly*, December 1987, p. 12.

8. "Eva Cardel Lowery Bowman Biographical Information," *Tennessee State University Online Archival*

Projects, <http://picard.tnstate.edu/~library/digital/bowbio.htm> (February 25, 1999).

Chapter 7. Giving to Others

1. A'Lelia Bundles, "Madam C. J. Walker," *American History*, August 1996, p. 48.

2. A'Lelia Perry Bundles, *Madam C. J. Walker, Entrepreneur* (New York: Chelsea House Publishers, 1991), p. 70.

3. Bundles, *American History*, p. 47.

4. Marion W. Taylor, *Madam C. J. Walker, Pioneer Businesswoman* (New York: Chelsea House Publishers, 1994), pp. 56–57.

5. David Levering Lewis, *When Harlem Was in Vogue* (New York: Penguin Books, 1997), pp. 9–10.

6. *Madam C. J. Walker: Entrepreneur, Philanthropist, Social Activist,* 1998, <http://www.madamcjwalker.com/> (February 25, 1999).

7. Lewis, p. 10.

8. Dorothy Hoobler and Thomas Hoobler, *The African-American Family Album* (New York: Oxford University Press, 1995), p. 82.

9. Paula Giddings, *When and Where I Enter* (New York: William Morrow and Company, 1984), p. 30.

10. Darlene Clark Hine and Kathleen Thompson, *A Shining Thread of Hope, The History of Black Women in America* (New York: Broadway Books, 1998), p. 206.

11. Library of Congress, "Influence of Prominent Abolitionists," *African-American Mosaic*, June 24, 1997, <http://lcweb.loc.gov/exhibits/african/afam006.html> (February 25, 1999).

12. Cookie Lommel, *Madam C. J. Walker Entrepreneur* (Los Angeles: Melrose Square Publishing Company, 1993), p. 126.

13. A'Lelia Perry Bundles, *Madam C. J. Walker, Entrepreneur* (New York: Chelsea House Publishers, 1991), p. 86.

Chapter 8. Villa Lewaro

1. Wilhelmena Robinson, *International Library of Negro Life and History: Historical Negro Biographies* (New York: Publishers Company, Inc., 1969), p. 138.

2. NPS, "Villa Lewaro," *Places Where Women Made History*, March 30, 1998, <http://www.cr.nps.gov/nr/travel/pwwmh/ny22.htm> (February 25, 1999).

3. A'Lelia Perry Bundles, *Madam C. J. Walker, Entrepreneur* (New York: Chelsea House Publishers, 1991), p. 95.

4. A'Lelia P. Bundles, "Madam C. J. Walker to Her Daughter A'Lelia Walker—The Last Letter," *Sage: A Scholarly Journal on Black Women*, Fall 1984, p. 35.

5. Ibid., p. 34.

6. A'Lelia P. Bundles, "Black Foremothers: Our Creative Trail Blazers," *Spelman Messenger*, vol. 101, Campus Issue, 1984, p. 19.

Chapter 9. A'Lelia and the Walker Company

1. Wilma L. Gibbs and Jill Landis, "Madam C. J. Walker Collection," *Indiana Historical Society*, August 13, 1993, <http://157.91.92.1/walker1.htm> (February 25, 1999).

2. Gale Group, "Madam C. J. Walker: Hairdresser, entrepreneur, and educational counselor," *DISCovering U.S. History on GaleNet*, 1999, <http://wale.gale.com/markets/schools/resrcs/womenhst/walkercj.htm> (February 25, 1999).

3. A'Lelia P. Bundles, "Madam C. J. Walker to Her Daughter A'Lelia Walker—The Last Letter," *Sage: A Scholarly Journal on Black Women*, Fall 1984, p. 35.

4. Cary D. Wintz, *Black Culture and the Harlem Renaissance* (Houston: Rice University Press, 1988), pp. 126–127.

5. David Levering Lewis, *When Harlem Was in Vogue* (New York: Penguin Books, 1997), pp. 166–167.

6. "Madame C. J. Walker Honored: The Rebirth of Walker Theatre Brings Celebs to Indianapolis," *Jet*, October 31, 1988, p. 62.

7. Lewis, pp. 265–266.

Chapter 10. The Memory and Legacy of Madam C. J. Walker

1. Nathan Aaseng, *Black Inventors* (New York: Facts on File, Inc., 1997), p. 84.

2. "Madame C. J. Walker Honored: The Rebirth of Walker Theatre Brings Celebs to Indianapolis," *Jet*, October 31, 1988, pp. 61–62.

3. *Madam C. J. Walker: Entrepreneur, Philanthropist, Social Activist*, 1998, <http://www.madamcjwalker.com/> (February 25, 1999).

4. Schlessinger Productions, *The Black Americans of Achievement Video Collection: Madam C. J. Walker* (Bala Cynwyd, Pa., 1992).

5. A'Lelia Bundles, "America's First Self-Made Woman Millionaire," *Radcliffe Quarterly*, December 1987, pp. 11–12.

6. A'Lelia Bundles, "Black Foremothers: Our Creative Trail Blazers," *Spelman Messenger*, vol. 101, Campus Issue, 1984, p. 19.

7. "Renovation Completed on Home of Madam C. J. Walker, America's First Black Woman Millionaire," *Jet*, August 14, 1995, p. 3.

8. Ibid.

9. Ibid., p. 4.

10. Bundles, "America's First Self-Made Woman Millionaire," p. 12.

11. A'Lelia Bundles, "Madam C. J. Walker," *American History*, August 1996, p. 48.

FURTHER READING

Bundles, A'Lelia Perry. *Madam C. J. Walker, Entrepreneur.* New York: Chelsea House Publishers, 1991.

Giddings, Paula. *When and Where I Enter: The Impact of Black Women on Race and Sex in America.* New York: William Morrow and Company, 1984.

Haskins, Jim. *One More River to Cross: The Stories of Twelve Black Americans.* New York: Scholastic, Inc., 1992.

Hoobler, Dorothy, and Thomas Hoobler. *The African-American Family Album.* New York: Oxford University Press, 1995.

Lewis, David Levering. *When Harlem Was in Vogue.* New York: Penguin Books, 1997.

Lommel, Cookie. *Madam C. J. Walker, Entrepreneur.* Los Angeles: Melrose Square Publishing Company, 1993.

Taylor, Marian W. *Madam C. J. Walker, Pioneer Businesswoman.* New York: Chelsea House Publishers, 1994.

Toby, Marlene. *Madam C. J. Walker, Pioneer Businesswoman.* New York: Children's Press, 1995.

ON THE INTERNET

Faces of Science: African Americans in the Sciences
<http://www.lib.lsu.edu/lib/chem/display/walker.html>

**Indiana Historical Society—
Madam C. J. Walker biographical sketch**
<http://157.91.92.1/madam.htm>

Madame C. J. Walker: Entrepreneur, Philanthropist, Social Activist
<http://www.madamcjwalker.com>

INDEX